FASTER

Adam Rapp

BROADWAY PLAY PUBLISHING INC
New York
www.broadwayplaypublishing.com
info@broadwayplaypublishing.com

FASTER
© Copyright 2004 Adam Rapp

All rights reserved. This work is fully protected under the copyright laws of the United States of America. No part of this publication may be photocopied, reproduced, stored in a retrieval system, or transmitted, in any form or by any means, electronic, mechanical, recording, or otherwise, without the prior permission of the publisher. Additional copies of this play are available from the publisher.

Written permission is required for live performance of any sort. This includes readings, cuttings, scenes, and excerpts. For amateur and stock performances, please contact Broadway Play Publishing Inc. For all other rights please contact the author c/o B P P I.

First Acting Edition: August 2020
I S B N: 978-0-88145-861-9

Book design: Marie Donovan
Page make-up: Adobe InDesign
Typeface: Palatino

FASTER was originally produced in New York City by the Rattlestick Theater Company (David Van Asselt, Artistic Director) at the Rattlestick Theater, opening on 9 September 2002. The cast was as follows:

STARGYL	Robert Beitzel
KITCHIN	Mtume Gant
SKRAM	Chris Messina
MAN	Roy Thinnes
GIRL	Fallone McDevitt Brooking
Director	Darrell Larson
Set design	David Korins
Costumes	Kaye Voyce
Lights	Jeff Croiter
Sound	Eric Shim
Production stage manager	Lori Ann Zepp

CHARACTERS & SETTING

STARGYL, *white, seventeen, starving, a mute*
KITCHIN, *black, barely twenty, starving, a dreamer*
SKRAM, *white, barely twenty, starving, a glue huffer,*
　STARGYL's *older brother*
MAN, *white; fiftyish, playful, terrifying*
GIRL, *a child from the river*

The basement room of a condemned apartment house.
Summer.

ACT ONE

(Twilight)

(The basement room of a condemned apartment house. A forgotten room. Malarial, spoiled walls. A crooked, half-collapsed staircase. A small, ceiling-level, foot-high drain window facing the street. A half-carpeted cement floor. Dirt. A door lading to a boiler room. A padlock securing the door.)

(Two thick heavy bag chains dangling from the ceiling, a large hook at the end of each chain. An ancient boxer's heavy bag leaning in one corner. Two makeshift sleeping nests against opposite walls. A metal sink. A broken section of mirror above the sink. A small jar of hair pomade next to the spout. A flashlight under the sink. An old radio whose reception phases in and out. A few wooden crates turned upside down as makeshift furniture. Several voided tubes of airplane glue scattered about the room. Random empty milk cartons and Count Chocula cereal boxes litter the floor. Strange squares torn in the milk cartons. A large plastic pink beach pail. A stack of newspapers neatly piled in one corner. The room is lit by a single filthy, naked bulb hanging from the center of the ceiling. A cheap transistor radio spits static and occasional decipherable bits.)

RADIO:
Florida orange juice on ice
Sounds so nice
In the morning

Florida orange juice on ice
Tastes so fresh
The day is dawning

Florida orange juice
Healthy start
To a brand new day

Florida orange juice
Vitamin C
It's the sunshine way

(STARGYL *is standing in the corner opposite the door to the boiler room. He is tall and thin, boyish. He is surrounded by a small shrine of green plastic toy soldiers. He is arranging them on the floor in various warfare poses, carefully removing them from a shoebox. He is dressed in a tattered seersucker suit, a white T-shirt underneath the jacket. He wears old high top sneakers, electric tape wrapped around the soles. On one hand he wears three plastic toy rings; cereal box prizes. Set neatly at his feet is a pair of enormous fire-engine-red pumps. He is sweating profusely. He occasionally barks at the flickering light. It is muffled but definitely a bark, more human than dog-like. The light continues to flicker. He covers his face with both hands as if trapped in a terrible storm. Outside, a broadcast public service announcement from a "Heat Relief" van.*)

BROADCAST: ATTENTION, ATTENTION. THIS IS THE AGENCY FOR HEAT RELIEF. IN LIGHT OF THE PRESENT CONDITIONS, DO NOT—I REPEAT—DO *NOT* PHYSICALLY EXERT YOURSELF. HEAT STROKE AND GENERAL EXHAUSTION ARE SERIOUS THREATS TO YOUR HEALTH.

(*The sound of descending footfalls.*)

(KITCHIN *enters from the staircase. He is black, barely twenty; thin. He wears a Chicago Bears football jersey and absurdly long basketball shorts. He has crude tattoos about his arms. On his feet he wears Nike basketball shoes. On his*

ACT ONE 3

head, a do rag. He carries a load of newspapers, a shoe-shine box on top of the papers. He dumps his load, taps the light. It stops flickering.)

KITCHIN: Yo, Stargyl, it's like a furnace out there. Sidewalk crackin. Street breathin up your legs. Can't even get no breeze from them big church fans at Saint Jack's. Feels like a dog's lickin you. Niggas sittin in the pews lookin like they meltin and shit. Women in they bras. Men naked from the waist up: Everyone starin at Jesus like he gonna do somethin about it. You know someone spray-painted that nigga blue? A blue motherfuckin Jesus. Like he a Smurf or some shit. That ain't right, Stargyl. This heat brings out the craziest shit in people. Liable to make a brother jump right in the river.

(The light flickers again. STARGYL *whimpers.)*

KITCHIN: Bellerin like a dog. It ain't nothin but a little light flickerin. You act like it's aliens or some shit.

*(*STARGYL *tries to force his hand in his mouth.)*

KITCHIN: Get your hand out your mouth.

*(*STARGYL *takes his hand out of his mouth.)*

KITCHIN: All you gotta do is tap that joint. *(He picks up one of the milk cartons, tears the lost child's photograph off the back panel, stares at it, takes a rubber-band-bound bunch of other milk carton photographs out of his pants, joins the new one with the others, stuffs the bunch down his pants.)* Pay phone ring?

*(*STARGYL *shakes his head.)*

KITCHIN: Yeah, that joint don't never ring. Skram said that nigga from Oswego's sposed to call.

*(*KITCHIN *picks up an empty tube of airplane glue, throws it against the wall.* STARGYL *starts to arrange his green plastic soldiers.)*

KITCHIN: Yeah, play with your army, Stargyl. Be all you can be and shit.

(STARGYL *plays. Static from the radio*)

KITCHIN: Yo, you been keepin lookout?

(STARGYL *nods.*)

KITCHIN: Defendin and watchdoggin? Woof-woofin like a good hound?

(STARGYL *nods, barks a few times.*)

KITCHIN: You didn't see no five-oh, did you? No pigs and chickens?

(STARGYL *shakes his head.*)

KITCHIN: None of them department of everlastin assbustin motherfuckas?

(*A knocking from behind the boiler room door*)

KITCHIN: It was Skram's turn to feed her. Punk-ass nigga never even came home last night. Knucklehead prolly got caught chasin paste. We was sposed to meet up at the train station. Trick a load of *Tribunes*. Talkin bout meet me at seven-thirty. Don't be late. Don't be a sucka. Motherfucka talkin about time in the A M and don't even got no watch!

Skram poppin off about gettin fifty heads from the janitor at the newspaper and shit. Sell em over at the train station to them rich white niggas on they way to Chi. I'm standin next to the switch house holdin a armful of yesterday's *Trib* lookin like I'm homeless and shit!

And you can't trick them white niggas twice cuz once they get to New Lennox they'll see it's yesterday's paper. Train hits Blue Island and they already callin the po-lice on they space phones.

Headlines is like the same every day, anyways. The heat-wave this. The reservoir that. Old folks dyin in

ACT ONE 5

fronta they fans. Skeighty-eighth day of no rain. Shit is gettin mad boring, yo. Motherfuckas get tired of readin bout the same old news. Lucky if we was to sell *half* them joints…

Skram's frantic ass! Janitor at the newspaper prolly busted him in the head with a push-broom.

Got my fitty from Big Cheese at the Copley printin press. Shine up his shoes and he always comes through for a brother. Got my fitty! (*He picks up a few empty boxes of Count Chocula, pours the d regs into the beach pail, stares at the small accumulation.*) Skram's fiendin-ass ate all the cereal again.

(*Another knock*)

(KITCHIN *picks up another tube of glue, throws the tube against the wall, more agitated. The light flickers again.*)

KITCHIN: You want the water?

(KITCHIN *grabs the plastic beach pail off the floor, crosses to the sink, dumps the cereal dregs, fills the pail with water. He crosses to* STARGYL, *holds the pail at his side.* STARGYL *reaches toward the pail with his ringed hand.*)

KITCHIN: Other hand, Stargyl. You wanna mess up your spook rings? Them joints won't glow right you get em wet.

(STARGYL *hesitates.*)

KITCHIN: Go head on and float your hand.

(STARGYL *places his other hand in the pail.* KITCHIN *swirls the water.*)

KITCHIN: That feel good?

(STARGYL *nods.*)

KITCHIN: I know it do. Like you in the pool over at Inwood. Jumpin off the divin board. Sink in down like you floatin through space. Touchin the bottom. All them locker keys caught in the drain. Maybe you see a quarter. You feelin it, right?

(STARGYL *nods.*)

KITCHIN: Yeah, B. *(Swirling the water)* Star-gyl. Stargyl Superstar! *(He stops swirling the water.)* You straight?

(STARGYL *nods.*)

KITCHIN: You frontin?

(STARGYL *shakes his head emphatically.*)

KITCHIN: No more actin like a little bitch, now. You start up again and I'll make you sit in the punk crate. Make you sit in that joint till Skram gets back, you hear?

(STARGYL *nods.* KITCHIN *crosses to the sink with the pail, dumps the water.* STARGYL *continues arranging his soldiers.* KITCHIN *crosses to a gym bag, gathers the small parts of his life, begins packing.* STARGYL *walks over; tries to stop him.*)

KITCHIN: What?

(STARGYL *points to his bag.*)

KITCHIN: Ain't nobody gonna leave you behind—you straight... *(Packing)* You packed up and ready to roll?

(STARGYL *nods.*)

KITCHIN: Got your comb?

(STARGYL *reaches into his pocket, removes a comb.*)

KITCHIN: Your lighter?

(STARGYL *reaches into his other pocket, removes a Zippo lighter.*)

KITCHIN: Star-gyl! Look at you! Tonight's the night, B. All this shit'll be settled. Finally pay off that Buick Electra two twenty-five over on Gompers. Buck and a half and it's ours. Two bills and Fat Rick throws in a extra set of Michelins.

… Money let me push that joint today. Shit was mad lovely, yo! Pleather interior. Electric seats. Power windows. Four-forty engine. Horse power buzzin all through my rib-cage. Niggas was like, *Whaddup, Kitchin? Where you get the ride, yo? Lemme sit shotgun*, and whatnot. Joint felted like I was ridin in some mad water-bed type shit.
Finally get the fuck off the East Side. Word is bond, Stargyl. So long as that nigga from Oswego come through.

(STARGYL *starts to comb his hair.*)

KITCHIN: Yeah, go head and do your hair. You do it good enough I'll give you some relaxer, bet?

(STARGYL *combs with concentration.*)

KITCHIN: Star-*gyl*! Stargyl Super*star*! Comb that shit, dog! Bust them naps! (*He crosses to the sink, grabs a small jar of pomade, applies it to* STARGYL's *hair.*) Skram says New York City but I say we lay it down in Florida. You ever seen Florida on the map, Stargyl? It look like a dick, B. Like big black donkey dick. Only they always make that joint yellow cuz of all the oranges and shit. They got mad vitamin C down there… (*He finishes with* STARGYL's *hair, picks up another box of cereal, peers inside.*) I'm starvin like marvin. Feels like motherfuckin cats is cryin in my stomach.
When I was at Saint Jack's Father Freeman told this Bible story about how Jesus made a school of fish appear in this dead river so all these homeless bummy-type niggas could eat. That sounds pretty dope, don't it, Stargyl?

(STARGYL *nods, still combing his hair.*)

KITCHIN: He said you can say this prayer. Somethin, somethin, I shall not want. The Lord is my Suburban or my Chevrolet or some shit. He said if you say it over and over it'll take that hunger away.

(KITCHIN *crosses to the boiler room door; presses his ear to it, then pushes away and starts walking frenetically around, like a caged animal, saying, "The Lord is my somethin but I shall not want. The Lord is my somethin but I shall not want," under his breath, clutching his sides.* STARGYL *combs his hair faster and faster; trying to keep pace with* KITCHIN.)

(*Again, outside a broadcast public service announcement from the "Heat Relief" van.*)

BROADCAST: ATTENTION, ATTENTION. THIS IS THE AGENCY FOR HEAT RELIEF. DUE TO THE CURRENT DRAUGHT, WATER LEVELS THROUGHOUT THE CITY ARE AT AN ALARMINGLY LOW LEVEL. PLEASE DO NOT! REPEAT—*DO NOT* FLUSH YOUR TOILET UNTIL FURTHER NOTICE.

(KITCHIN *crosses to the sink, lowers his head over the faucet, lifts his do rag, runs cold water over the back of his neck, stops the faucet, then crosses to the window, jumps up, grabs the ledge, pulls himself up, peers out.*)

KITCHIN: Come on, Skram! ...Where is that nigga?! Fiendin-ass paste-head. (*He lets himself down, picks up a box of Count Chocula, shakes it, drops the box, picks up another; shakes it, throws it to the floor.*) I don't know about that nigga, sometimes, Stargyl. Got all these ideas, but don't none of them ever work out. Snatchin headlines. Jukin quarters from pay phones. Scrappin car parts over on Plainfield Road.

Don't none of it ever pay. And if it do it ain't shit but enough for a train ticket to Chi. We get there we can't do nothin cuz we broke. Wind up ridin the El all night. Memorizin all the stops on the Red Line. Knowin them joints backwards and shit. Thinkin about gettin a drink.

ACT ONE

Gettin some ass. Nothin but them South Side hos on the train stankin up the seats with they rotten pussies. Shoulda spent the summer in Rock Island with my cousin Two Tone. Sells T-shirts out the back of his Nova. Mickey Mouse and shit. I'm with stupid and whatnot. At least people buy them joints. Two Tone's got a tough little crib, too. Color TV Microwave. Nice hot shower.

Rock Island woulda been better than this shit. Always waitin around for nothin. Growin old like them lopsided niggas at O T B. Money from Oswego better show.

(Suddenly, rapid footfalls descending the stairs. STARGYL *starts to bark.* SKRAM *enters in a whirlwind, a large paperboy bag slung over his shoulder. He is barely twenty, white, very thin, very pale. He has a very short crew cut. He wears a New York Knicks away jersey over a white T-shirt, absurdly long basketball shorts, and Timberland boots. There are crude tattoos about his arms.* STARGYL *stops barking.* SKRAM *runs to the window, jumps to grab the ledge, pulls himself up.)*

SKRAM: You chasin a ghost, G! *(Siren)* Woo-woo-woo! Flatfooted faggits! *(He laughs, taps on the window, lets himself down.)* Got them jokers chasin they tails at the Jewel and shit. Popsicles poppin out the box. Push-ups and Drumsticks rollin down the aisles. T V dinners slidin everywhere. Security guards breakin they ankles in the frozen food section. Pack my bag, jump the turnstile, and I'm ghost, G.

Jet down Jefferson. Catch a green light at six corners. Another oh so friendly green on Black Road. I'm just a paperboy makin my route, clockin my time. Shit, Count Chocula's gettin simpler and simpler. Whaddup, yo?

(KITCHIN *and* SKRAM *tap fists, though* KITCHIN *is reluctant.* SKRAM *crosses to* STARGYL *holds his fist out, greeting him.*)

SKRAM: Star-gyl. Whaddup, G?

(STARGYL *stares at his fist.*)

SKRAM: Gimme a pound, yo!

(STARGYL *stares at his fist, taps it.*)

(*From his bag,* SKRAM *removes two boxes of* Count Chocula *and a quart of milk, sets them on a crate, crosses to the sink, grabs the plastic beach pail, opens a box of cereal, pours its entirety into the pail, empties the quart of milk into the pail, pulls a small plastic beach shovel out of the back of his shorts, wolfs down the cereal.*)

SKRAM: Hot as a motherfucker out there, G! Cars parked with they windows open. People sittin in front of they cribs flappin the newspaper. Lookin like they don't got no blood in they bodies. Tables. Chairs. Half the kitchen in the front yard. Niggas down by the river just standin in the mud. Standin all still like they waitin for somethin. It's like a hundred and twenty degrees out and shit.

KITCHIN: Where was you, B?

SKRAM: *(Eating)* Where was I when, G?

KITCHIN: At seven motherfuckin thirty, that's when! I waited for you at the switch house for forty-five solid. Walkie-talkie nigga comes out askin me what I'm doin and shit. I'm holdin my fitty yesterdays like I'm tryin to sell the paper to the train tracks!

SKRAM: Aw, snap. My bad, Kitchin. I forgot.

KITCHIN: You forgot?

SKRAM: (*crossing to sink, cooling off, checking himself in the mirror*) I had other business.

ACT ONE

KITCHIN: Other business.

SKRAM: Yeah, G. Other *bid*ness.

KITCHIN: Like what kind of *bid*ness.

SKRAM: Like bidness of the other variety.

KITCHIN: You was chasin paste!

SKRAM: I wasn't chasin no paste, yo. I told you I stopped wif that nonsense.

KITCHIN: Man, you ain't stopped nothin. *(He picks up a voided tube of glue off the floor, throws it at* SKRAM.*)*

SKRAM: I'm tellin you I stopped, G. Shit started makin me dream funny. Dreamin bout sharks and whatnot. And they wasn't no regular-type T V sharks, yo. They was like sharks that can walk around and drive cars. Fuckin Calamityville Horror type joints. Chasin me down Gompers in sharkmobiles.

KITCHIN: That shit don't do nothin but make you paranoid.

SKRAM: Takes them hunger pains away.

KITCHIN: That's why that nigga Blue Tip started duckin all the time. He always think someone be tryin to push him from behind. That's that pastehead paranoia. I'd rather *feel* my hunger. I'm starvin, I'm starvin. I don't need to pretend and shit.

(SKRAM *moves to the entrance to the boiler room, presses his ear to the door.* KITCHIN *crosses to* STARGYL *with the pail of cereal and the shovel. He hands the pail to* STARGYL, *who lifts it to his face and drinks the rest.)*

SKRAM: Anyone come through?

KITCHIN: I ain't hip. Just got back my damn self

SKRAM: Anybody come through, Stargyl? Any pigs and chickens?

(STARGYL *shakes his head.)*

SKRAM: *(To* STARGYL*)* You shit your pants again? *(To* KITCHIN*)* He shit his pants again?

KITCHIN: Naw, B.

SKRAM: *(Kicking* STARGYL*'s army men, they go flying)* I'm gonna have to scrape some fuckin Pampers for his intercontinental ass.

(STARGYL *retrieves his army men, resets them.*)

KITCHIN: I said he didn't shit his pants, yo. And it's in*con*tinent.

SKRAM: Yeah, you know, right?

KITCHIN: I do know. I ain't the one who can't read.

SKRAM: Condiments. Consonants. Condolences. It's all the same to me. *(To* STARGYL*)* Intercontinental bitch-ass nigga. *(Crossing to* STARGYL*)* Why was he cryin?

KITCHIN: He wasn't cryin.

SKRAM: His face is wet!

KITCHIN: He just nervous and shit.

SKRAM: Nervous little punk.

KITCHIN: The light was going funny again.

SKRAM: Retarded crumbum sissy. Cryin at the light.

KITCHIN: Leave him be, yo. You know he gets amped about that simple shit.

SKRAM: Faggit! You wanna see my dick, bitch? *(Taking his penis out)* Biggest dick in the world, G. You wanna touch it?

(STARGYL *starts to cry.* SKRAM *laughs, stuffs his penis back in his pants.*)

SKRAM: Put your sissy shoes on.

(STARGYL *doesn't move.*)

SKRAM: I said put em on, bitch!

(STARGYL *removes his rotten sneakers and slips into the red pumps.*)

SKRAM: Dance like a ho.

(STARGYL *is frozen.*)

SKRAM: Dance like a ho, nigga!

KITCHIN: C'mon, Skram. Stop with that shit, yo!

SKRAM: I want him to dance like the bitch he is, G. Look at him.

KITCHIN: Shit is mad unnecessary, B.

SKRAM: It ain't even your motherfuckin business, Kitchin. Dance, Stargyl!

(STARGYL *pulls his pants up slightly revealing the pumps and his filthy ankles. He starts to dance very slowly, awkwardly.* SKRAM *claps a slow cadence.*)

SKRAM: Go head on, ho. Do your sissy dance.

(SKRAM *claps faster and faster.* STARGYL *crudely dances, trying to match the velocity of his claps.*)

SKRAM: Woo-woo-woo!

(KITCHIN *takes the pail back from* STARGYL, *crosses to the sink, rinses it out.*)

SKRAM: Stop dancin.

(STARGYL *bends down to remove the pumps.*)

SKRAM: Did I say take em off?

(STARGYL *stops.* KITCHIN *fills the beach pail with water and crosses to* STARGYL. *He takes his hand, puts it in the water, swirls it.*)

KITCHIN: *(To* SKRAM*)* What the fuck is wrong with you, B?!

SKRAM: He *my* brother, G.

KITCHIN: Treatin him like a little bitch!

SKRAM: *(Indignant)* What?

KITCHIN: What, *what,* nigga! That shit is like child abuse, yo!

SKRAM: Stargyl knows I loves him.

(SKRAM *crosses to* STARGYL, *fluffs his hair.*)

SKRAM: Star-*gyl*. Stargyl Super*star*. My nigga.

(STARGYL *smiles.*)

SKRAM: See? *(He fake boxes him in the ribs.)* Who's your nigga, Stargyl? Who's your nigga? *(He fluffs his hair again.)*

KITCHIN: He think we leavin him behind.

SKRAM: We *should* leave his doofy-ass behind.

(KITCHIN *takes the pail away, crosses to the sink, dumps the water.* SKRAM *crosses to the entrance to the boiler room, presses his ear to the door, pushes away, lies down.* STARGYL *continues to rearrange his army men.*)

SKRAM: Money from Oswego call yet?

KITCHIN: Payphone's broke, yo.

SKRAM: No it ain't. You just gotta hit that bitch. Blue Tip called me earlier. Joint was ringin loud and clear. Sounded like a ho screamin for her pussy back. *Give it back, Skram! Give it back!*

KITCHIN: Nigga from Oswego still talkin two gees?

SKRAM: Shit, three. Maybe four he likes what he sees. Four gees, Kitchin. That's mad currency.

KITCHIN: I'm hip.

SKRAM: Mad, made-in-the-shade, drink-lemonade type bank.

KITCHIN: Yo, Fat Rick let me push the Electra today.

SKRAM: Word?

ACT ONE 15

KITCHIN: Word is bond, B. Shit was mad lovely.

(SKRAM *motions to* KITCHIN, KITCHIN *reaches into his shoeshine box, throws* SKRAM *a shoe brush.* SKRAM *brushes his Timberland boots.*)

KITCHIN: Buck and a half and it's ours. Two bills and he throws in a new set of Michelins.

SKRAM: Finally get the fuck outta this heat. Away from this nowhere-ass town.

KITCHIN: Nowhere-ass, ho-infested, pastehead *tizz*own.

SKRAM: I'm tired of being one of these East Side river niggas that don't never get over the Hill. One day you twenty, the next thing you know you skeighty-eight and sportin the same burnt sneakers.

KITCHIN: Same old broke-ass kicks and shit.

(*Again, outside, a broadcast public service announcement from the "Heat Relief" van.*)

BROADCAST: ATTENTION, ATTENTION. THIS IS THE AGENCY FOR HEAT RELIEF. IT HAS BEEN BROUGHT TO OUR AWARENESS THAT THE FIRE HYDRANT ON THE CORNER OF JEFFERSON STREET AND GOMPERS BOULEVARD IS CONTAMINATED. UNIDENTIFIED BACTERIA HAS BEEN DISCOVERED FROM THIS WATER SOURCE. DO NOT DRINK THE WATER FROM THE FIRE HYDRANT ON THE CORNER OF JEFFERSON STREET AND GOMPERS BOULEVARD. I REPEAT, DO NOT DRINK THE WATER FROM THE FIRE HYDRANT ON THE CORNER OF JEFFERSON STREET AND GOMPERS BOULEVARD.

(SKRAM *crosses to the window, drops the shoe brush back in* KITCHIN'*s box, pulls himself up to the window, peers out, lets himself down, crosses to the sink, falls down, gets back up, whirls.*)

SKRAM: Why you pushin me?

KITCHIN: What?

SKRAM: You pushed me.

KITCHIN: I ain't even near you, nigga.

SKRAM: Why you pushin me, Stargyl?

KITCHIN: Nigga, please. He all the way over in the corner... Someone prolly been "pushin" you a *lot* lately.

SKRAM: Pushin me and callin me Larry. I think someone at the Jewel was whisperin that shit in my ear.

KITCHIN: I'm tellin you that's that paste fuckin with you, B.

SKRAM: Last nigga who called me Larry got a fork in his neck. *(Turns to the door)* You feed her yet?

KITCHIN: You was sposed to feed her this mornin.

SKRAM: Aw, you didn't feed her, Kitchin?

KITCHIN: Feed her what, B? You keep eatin all the Count Chocula. Shit's sposed to be for her, yo. Fiendin-ass nigga.

SKRAM: I just brought two more boxes.

KITCHIN: You ain't *brought* shit. You scraped them joints.

SKRAM: Brought em, scraped em. What's the difference, G?

KITCHIN: Hooligan-ass bitch.

SKRAM: Suck on these nuts.

KITCHIN: Someday they gonna catch you, Skram. Throw you in the tank with the sharks and the troublefish. Have that ass bent over the foosball table.

ACT ONE

(SKRAM *crosses to the unopened box of Count Chocula, throws it to* KITCHIN. KITCHIN *catches it, throws it back to* SKRAM.)

SKRAM: I said ain't feedin her.

KITCHIN: Sissy.

SKRAM: Thought you likeded feedin her.

KITCHIN: Thought light lit. Thought you farted but you shit.

SKRAM: The other day you said it was cool cuz it made you feel *hard*. You gotta feed her, yo.

KITCHIN: I don't *gotta* do shit!

SKRAM: She don't even look at me, Kitchin.

KITCHIN: That's cuz you be scarin her. Poppin off about "Who's your parents! Who's your parents!" Snappin matches at her.

SKRAM: Little-ass ho just sits there in the dark like that shit don't bother her. Ain't nuffin in her eyes. It's like starin into some bullet holes. And she don't even speak, yo. You feed her.

KITCHIN: I didn't like that shit last time, okay?

SKRAM: You didn't *like* it.

KITCHIN: Naw, B. Somethin about it wasn't right.

SKRAM You goin soft, Kitchin? Spendin too much time wif that priestly nigga over at Saint Jack's. Wipin off bingo cards. Readin the dictionary. What's his name—Father Feelgood and shit?

KITCHIN: Father *Freeman*, knucklehead.

SKRAM: Father Feelgood poppin that Jesus word. I saw you over there again today. Moppin the floor. Changin the holy water.

KITCHIN: Man, I was over there cuz they got them big church fans. All types of people was. Only place you can go to get out the heat, B.

SKRAM: Uh-huh.

KITCHIN: Nigga, all the air conditioners in the city is like mad busted!

SKRAM: Not the one at the Jewel.

KITCHIN: Well I wasn't over by there.

SKRAM: Or the one at the *car lot*. Fat Rick had that joint mad pumpin, Kitchin. Gave me goose pimples and shit. Over at Saint Jack's moppin the floor like a ho.

KITCHIN: Nigga, they be givin out free donuts at St. Jack's and you know it!

SKRAM: Pretty soon you'll be singin in the choir like a little bitch. Our Father who farts in heaven and shit. Father Feelgood'll be takin your temperature. Forcin his holy thermometer up your black ass... And what the fuck was doin on the train bridge?

KITCHIN: What?

SKRAM: I saw you up there.

KITCHIN: I was just lookin down at the water. Why the fuck you following me anyway?

SKRAM: Kitchin's going soft on us, Stargyl. When we get to New York I'm gonna have to find him some bitch panties. Some New York Knicks hotpants and shit.

KITCHIN: *(Pointing to the boiler room)* This ain't even about bein soft, Skram. We shouldn'ta took her. We start off jukin quarters and stealin scratch tickets and now we fuckin kidnappin little kids!

SKRAM: All sweet and tender like a applesnap. My little black buttery applesnap. *(Smooches the air)*

ACT ONE 19

KITCHIN: Man, *fuck* you.

SKRAM: Maybe Stargyl'll feed her. *(To* STARGYL*)* You wanna feed her, Stargyl? Bitch-ass Kitchin's gain soft on us.

*(*STARGYL *starts to cry.)*

KITCHIN: See, now look whatchu gone and done.

SKRAM: *(To* STARGYL*)* You better eat that shit!

*(*STARGYL *stops crying.)*

SKRAM: Faggit-ass ho.

*(*SKRAM *takes* STARGYL*'s rings off his fingers, throws them across the room.)*

KITCHIN: *You* go in there you so brave.

SKRAM: Choose for it.

KITCHIN: *Choose* for it?

SKRAM: Yeah, G. It's democratic and shit.

KITCHIN: And we a democracy, right?

SKRAM: Kitchin, Skram, and Stargyl, yo. Stars and Stripes forever.

KITCHIN: I got odds.

SKRAM: Odd motherfucker.

KITCHIN & SKRAM: Once, twice, three, shoot.

*(*KITCHIN *and* SKRAM *both throw two fingers.* KITCHIN *loses.)*

KITCHIN: Punk.

*(*KITCHIN *takes the box of cereal, opens it, and pours the contents into the beach pail. A small plastic toy ring falls out. He picks it up off the floor, puts it in his pocket. He pours the carton of milk into the pail, sets the pail down, tears the new lost child photo off the back panel, stares at it for a moment, removes the bunch of pictures from his shorts,*

joins the new one with the others, returns the bunch to the inside of his shorts, retrieves the pail.)

(SKRAM *crosses to* STARGYL, *reaches under his T-shirt, removes the shoelace key necklace, crosses to the entrance to the boiler room, inserts the key, unlocks the padlock, waves his hand at the door like a concierge.)*

(KITCHIN *grabs the flashlight from under the sink, slowly crosses to the entrance to the boiler room.)*

KITCHIN: You got another spoon?

(SKRAM *reaches into his shorts, removes another plastic beach shovel, drops it into the beach pail, opens the door.* KITCHIN *exits into the boiler room.* SKRAM *closes the door, sets the padlock in the hasp but does not lock it, then crosses to* STARGYL, *tucks the shoelace key necklace back under his shirt, crosses to the sink, cools off.* STARGYL *steps across his shrine of army men, retrieves one of the torn milk cartons. As he is retrieving the milk cartons,* SKRAM *flings water at him playfully.* STARGYL *crosses back to his corner, smiling, stands.)*

SKRAM: Yo, Stargyl. Guess who I thought I saw today? You ain't even gonna believe me, Superstar. I'll give you one guess… Stand up straight, ho!

(STARGYL *stands taller.)*

SKRAM: That's right. You guessed it: Mommy. Disco Jean. Disco Jean the Dancin Machine. Thought she was locked up and shit, right? *(He crosses to his paperboy bag, removes a fresh tube of airplane glue.)* This bitch is walkin down the Hill, lookin like a fat-ass dolphin. Cracka her ass switchin in the breeze. Pussy stankin up the sidewalk. Drivin dogs under porches. Birds into barbecue pits. Her feet comin outta her stilettos. Fishnet stockins runnin everywhere. Breakin her ankles all the way down the Hill and shit. Disco Jean the Dancin Machine. Some old lopsided nigga from

ACT ONE 21

the bowlin alley trailin behind her all slow and careful. Panama hat. Big-ass collar flappip in the wind. Tryin to be slick like he ain't goin for some. Charlie Customer and shit. I'm like, *"Disco Jean! Disco Jean the Dancin Machine! Yo, Mommy!"*
She gets into a Lincoln Clown Car at the corner of Gompers and Jackson, right? Nigga wif the collar gets in after her. Takes his hat off before he opens the door like he a real gentleman and shit. They ride off down Jackson. Turn left on Truesdale. She prolly still lickin that nigga's butthole.
Thought for sure it was her but it wasn't. Crackhead ho.

(SKRAM *unscrews the glue, snorts it into each nostril, crawls over to the staircase, takes his pants down, starts to masturbate on his knees, facing the shadows. He comes, takes a few deep breaths, rises, stomps out his mess into the floor, turns to* STARGYL.)

SKRAM: What?

(SKRAM *moves to the heavy bag and starts to punch it violently. He counts out with each punch.* STARGYL *starts to cry.* SKRAM *reaches thirty-three, stops punching the heavy bag, paces around the room, catching his breath.*)

SKRAM: Quit cryin, ho!

(STARGYL *tries to stop crying.* SKRAM *pulls a lollipop out of the paperboy bag, removes the wrapper.*)

SKRAM: Keep cryin and I ain't givin it to you. It's root beer, too, Pussy. *(Holding out the lollipop)* Is this how you gonna be in New York City? If I get a job wif the Knicks how the fuck am I gonna get you hired if you can't act a like a man? They don't let sissies sell popcorn at Madison Square Garden, Stargyl.

(STARGYL *stop crying.* SKRAM *hands him the lollipop.* STARGYL *puts it in his mouth.*)

SKRAM: Good, right? Joint prolly melted and shit. So fuckin hot out.

(SKRAM *paces, crosses to* STARGYL, *lifts his left pant leg, revealing a small snub-nosed .22 caliber revolver strapped to his calf* SKRAM *removes the revolver, holds it up to the light, unlocks the chamber, spins the carriage, stops it, counts the bullets, pops the carriage back in, locks the chamber, spins it in his hand, aims at the heavy bag.)*

SKRAM: What? ...What?! ...You late, motherfucka. I said you *late*! Blop, blop, blop! *(He holds his aim. To the heavy bag)* Woo-woo-woo! Punk-ass nigga. *(He spins it in his hand again, then points it at* STARGYL.*)*

(A knocking from the boiler room. SKRAM *turns to it, startled, then laughs, crosses to* STARGYL, *re-sets the gun on his leg.)*

KITCHIN: Open the door, yo!

*(*SKRAM *knocks back at* KITCHIN, *laughing. A momentary cacophony of knocking.* SKRAM *stops, opens the door.* KITCHIN *rushes out, falls to the floor, vomits into the floor drain.)*

(Again, outside, a broadcast public service announcement from the "Heat Relief" van.)

BROADCAST: ATTENTION, ATTENTION. THIS IS THE AGENCY FOR HEAT RELIEF. PLEASE KEEP YOUR SMALL CHILDREN OUT OF THE RIVER. I REPEAT, PLEASE KEEP YOUR SMALL CHILDREN OUT OF THE RIVER.

KITCHIN: She talked to me.

SKRAM: She did?

KITCHIN: I ain't lyin, B. Her voice is bug, yo.

SKRAM: Bug like what?

KITCHIN: Bug like that shit ain't even comin from inside her.

ACT ONE 23

SKRAM: Where's it comin from?

KITCHIN: Somewhere else.

(SKRAM *laughs, makes silly Twilight Zone sounds.*)

KITCHIN: She told me she came from the river, Skram!

SKRAM: The *river*.

KITCHIN: She said she was borned in the belly of a fish.

SKRAM: Be serious, yo.

KITCHIN: That's what she said.

SKRAM: Who is she, fuckin Shark Girl or some shit?

KITCHIN: Think about it, Skram.

SKRAM: Think about what, Kitchin?

KITCHIN: You found her down by the casino boat.

SKRAM: So?

KITCHIN: *(Removes the milk carton pictures from his shorts)* We ain't seen her on no milk carton. Or none of them posters on the telephone poles. She said some other bugged-out shit, too. Some biblical type shit.

SKRAM: *(Teasing)* Some biblical, apocalyptical type nonsense?

KITCHIN: She told me that this big-ass storm is comin. That it's gonna rain so hard the river's gonna start flowin backwards.

SKRAM: Comin when?

KITCHIN: Tonight, B!

SKRAM: It ain't rained in mad weeks, G. The sidewalks on Gompers is like crackin from the heat. *(Crosses to boiler room door)* Since when did that little ho start talkin?

KITCHIN: I ain't hip. I guess today.

SKRAM: So she like a weatherman?

KITCHIN: She somethin.

SKRAM: She a little *kid*, Kitchin!

KITCHIN: Skram, she told me the rain's gonna change to flies and that the flies is gonna change to fire!

SKRAM: Like Indiana Jones and the Temple of Gloom and whatnot.

KITCHIN: What if it's true?

SKRAM: That shit is *bananas*, yo!

KITCHIN: She said the fish will protect us.

SKRAM: The *who*?

KITCHIN: The fish, B. The fish.

SKRAM: What fish?

KITCHIN: Fuck if I know!

SKRAM: Protect us from what?

KITCHIN: Prolly some seriously gloomy shit.

SKRAM: That sounds kinda dope, yo. Like some mad science fiction type nonsense. Stargyl, don't that sound dope?

KITCHIN: We should put her back, Skram.

SKRAM: Put her back! Put her back where, Kitchin-the supermarket? The fuckin shoppin mall?

KITCHIN: The river.

SKRAM: You seriously trippin, G.

(The sound of distant thunder. KITCHIN *and* SKRAM *stare up, then turn to each other.)*

SKRAM: She do look kinda spooky, don't she?

KITCHIN: I'm hip, B.

SKRAM: All white and shit.

KITCHIN: Nowhere-ass lookin eyes.

ACT ONE 25

KITCHIN & SKRAM: Like she came from a fish, G/B.

(*Again, distant thunder.* KITCHIN *and* SKRAM *stare at each other a long moment, then* KITCHIN *starts for the stairs.*)

SKRAM: Where you goin, Kitchin?

(KITCHIN *exits up the stairs.* SKRAM *follows him halfway up.*)

SKRAM: You comin back, right?!

(*No answer.* SKRAM *comes back down, paces a moment, falls to the floor, gets back up, whirls.*)

SKRAM: Why you pushin me, Stargyl?!

(STARGYL *takes a step back.* SKRAM *dusts himself off, looks around. Rolling thunder.* STARGYL *tries to swallow his hand.*)

SKRAM: Get your hand out your mouth! Ain't nothin but a little thunder. Punk-ass nigga. *Should* leave you here.

(STARGYL *takes his hand out of his mouth.*)

SKRAM: Put your sissy shoes back on!

(*The sound of a payphone ringing.* SKRAM *makes a dead sprint for the staircase, exits up the stairs. The payphone rings a few more times, then ceases.* STARGYL *stands very still in the corner.*)

(*Again, approaching thunder*)

(*A knocking from within.* STARGYL *stares at the entrance to the boiler room.*)

(*More knocking*)

(STARGYL *crosses to the entrance of the boiler room. The light starts to flicker. He stares at it.*)

(*More knocking*)

(STARGYL *turns to the door, reaches under his shirt, removes the shoelace key necklace. He inserts the key into the lock, unlocks it, removes the lock, quickly retreats to his corner, behind his plastic army. The light flickers. He turns and faces the corner.)*

(The light stops flickering.)

(The boiler room door opens and a GIRL *appears in the entrance, She might be six or seven. There is a small section of silver duct tape covering her mouth. On one hand, she wears a plastic toy ring, the prize from a Count Chocula cereal box.)*

*(*STARGYL *turns, stares at her curiously, crosses to her. She motions to him to go to his knees. He does so.)*

(The GIRL *removes the ring from her finger, places it on* STARGYL's *pinkie. He stares at all his rings, smiles.)*

(The GIRL *reaches under her dress and removes a small fish, hands it to* STARGYL. *He holds the fish in his hand for a long moment, smiles.)*

(He reaches into his back pocket, removes his comb, hands it to her. She takes the comb, runs it through her hair a few times, hands it back. He urges her to keep the comb. She runs the comb through his hair a few times, hands the comb back, he puts it back into his pocket. She holds her hand out as if to ask for something else. STARGYL *reaches into his other pocket, removes the Zippo lighter, opens the top, flicks at it. She shakes her head, keeps her hand out.* STARGYL *returns the Zippo to his pocket, pulls up his pant leg, revealing the revolver. She nods.)*

(He removes the revolver, hands it to her. She keeps it in his hand, turns the nose toward her chest. He pulls the revolver back, shakes his head.)

(She pulls the nose of the gun toward her again, he pulls back again, puts it back into the leg strap very quickly, slips the pant leg over the gun.)

(She waves at him to bend down again. He does. She closes his eyes with her finger tips. She removes the section of duct tape, sings.)

GIRL: *(Singing)*
Florida orange juice on ice
Sounds so nice
In the morning

Florida orange juice on ice
Tastes so fresh
The day is dawning

Florida orange juice
Healthy start
To a brand new day

Florida orange juice
Vitamin C
It's the sunshine way

(She kisses both of his eyes, re-sets the duct tape back over her mouth, and then turns and crosses to the boiler room. The door closes behind her.)

(STARGYL opens his eyes, stares at the fish in his hand.)

(The light begins flickering again.)

(STARGYL places the fish in his interior breast pocket, crosses to the boiler room entrance, re-padlocks the door, but doesn't lock it. He crosses to the corner, stands very still.)

(The light continues to flicker.)

(He crosses to the sink, grabs the plastic beach pail, runs the water, fills the pail, sets the pail in the center of the room, removes the fish from his interior breast pocket, stares at it in his hand for a moment, drops it into the pail, turns, crosses back to his corner, stands very still.)

(Footfalls descending the staircase. KITCHIN enters, He is holding a single donut wrapped in a napkin. He crosses to STARGYL, gives him the donut.)

KITCHIN: The Lord is my shepherd, I shall not want, Stargyl. That's that joint! The Lord is my shepherd, I shall not want. It's a Psalm, see? *(He removes a piece of torn paper from his shorts.)* It's a Psalm of David. Psalm twenty-three and shit. *(Reciting from the paper)* The Lord is my shepherd; I shall not want. He maketh me to lie down in green pastures; He leadeth me beside the still waters. Sounds like he on a motherfuckin golf course, don't it? He restoreth my soul; He guideth me in straight paths for His name's sake. Yea, though I walk through the valley of the shadow of death, I will fear no evil, for Thou art with me; Thy rod and Thy staff, they comfort me. He must be sportin a gat or some shit. Thou preparest a table before me in the presence of mine enemies; Thou hast a…nointed my head with oil; my cup runneth over. Surely goodness and mercy shall follow me all the days of my life; and I shall dwell in the house of the Lord for ever.
I don't even know what that shit means, yo, but Father Freeman said you just keep sayin that joint over and over.

(STARGYL nods, eats the donut.)

(The sound of violent rain. KITCHIN starts to pace around the room, reciting the prayer feverishly. He looks down, sees the beach pail, stops.)

KITCHIN: What the fuck is that, yo? *(He bends down, jumps back)* Stargyl, you see that?

(STARGYL nods. Loud thunder)

KITCHIN: Where'd it come from, B?

(STARGYL shakes his head. A flash of lightning in the window)

(STARGYL covers his eyes. KITCHIN continues to stare at the fish. Descending footfalls. SKRAM enters in a sprint for the sink, vomits.)

ACT ONE

SKRAM: *(At sink)* Phone rang.

KITCHIN: *(Still staring into the bucket)* Cat from Oswego?

SKRAM: Uh-huh.

KITCHIN: You talk to him?

SKRAM: Yeah, I talked to that nigga. Money's got a bug voice, yo.

KITCHIN: Bug like what?

SKRAM: Bug like when he was talkin it was like it wasn't comin through the phone.

KITCHIN: Where was it comin from?

SKRAM: It was like his voice was everywhere, G. Like that shit was inside you.

KITCHIN: He on his way?

SKRAM: *(Turning, facing* KITCHIN*)* Yeah, he on his way.

(The sound of thunder, KITCHIN *turns to* SKRAM. *They look up at the window.)*

SKRAM: It's rainin sideways, yo. Like it's chasin you and shit. Ain't never seen nothin like it, Kitchin. And the river…

KITCHIN: What about the river?

SKRAM: Shit is runnin backwards, G.

KITCHIN: Word?

SKRAM: Word is bond.

KITCHIN: Yo, Skram. This cat from Oswego. The dude with the voice. ..

SKRAM: Uh-huh.

KITCHIN: He still talkin four gees?

SKRAM: Nigga's poppin some new shit.

KITCHIN: Yeah? What type of shit is that?

SKRAM: Like some genie-in-a-bottle type nonsense. He said we could have whatever we want.

KITCHIN: Whatever we want.

SKRAM: As in anything there is.

KITCHIN: Damn.

SKRAM: I know. Damn. Nigga must got mad loot.

KITCHIN: Mad somethin…

(The light starts flickering, KITCHIN *crosses to the bucket.)*

SKRAM: What's in the pail?

KITCHIN: Huh?

SKRAM: The pail, G. You starin at it like it's talking to you and shit.

KITCHIN: You ain't even gonna believe me.

SKRAM: Why not?

KITCHIN: I think it's a shark, Skram.

SKRAM: A *shark*?

KITCHIN: A little baby shark. Shit is seriously bug, yo.

SKRAM: Do it got teef?

KITCHIN: Mad vampire type joints.

(SKRAM crosses to the beach pail, looks inside.)

SKRAM: This shit is bananas, Kitchin.

KITCHIN: I'm hip.

(Loud thunder. SKRAM *sees that the padlock isn't closed, rushes to the door, locks it.)*

KITCHIN: You straight, Stargyl?

(STARGYL nods.)

KITCHIN: You sure?

(STARGYL nods. A flash of lightning)

ACT ONE

KITCHIN: This shit is bug, right?

(STARGYL *nods.*)

KITCHIN: You still got your comb?

(STARGYL *nods*).

KITCHIN: You wanna do your hair?

(STARGYL *shakes his head.*)

KITCHIN: You don't?

(*The light starts to flicker again.*)

KITCHIN: Stargyl…Stargyl Super*star*.

(*Again, outside, a broadcast public service announcement from the "Heat Relief" van.*)

BROADCAST: ATTENTION, ATTENTION. THIS IS THE AGENCY FOR HEAT RELIEF. THERE IS A FLASH FLOOD WARNING IN EFFECT. HEAVY RAINS AND ELECTRICAL STORMS ARE IMMINENT! DO NOT GO OUTSIDE. I REPEAT, WHATEVER YOU DO, DO NOT GO OUTSIDE!

(STARGYL *bends down and grabs two army men from his shrine. He crosses to* SKRAM *and* KITCHIN, *hands one to each, crosses back to his spot in the corner.* SKRAM *and* KITCHIN *stare at the army men.*)

(*The light is still flickering.* SKRAM *crosses to the light, taps it. It blows to total darkness. A flash of lightning*)

SKRAM'S VOICE: Oh, shit…

END OF ACT ONE

ACT TWO

(Total darkness)
(The sound of breathing)
SKRAM'S VOICE: *(A whisper)* Kitchin…
(No response)
SKRAM'S VOICE: *(A whisper)* Hey, Kitchin.
(No response)
SKRAM'S VOICE: YO, KITCHIN!
KITCHIN'S VOICE: What, nigga?!
SKRAM'S VOICE: I was callin you, G!
KITCHIN'S VOICE: I heard you.
SKRAM'S VOICE: So answer then, bitch!
KITCHIN'S VOICE: *(Swallowing)* My mouth was full.
SKRAM'S VOICE: Fulla what?
KITCHIN'S VOICE: I ain't hip. It tasted like a apple.
SKRAM'S VOICE: A *apple*!
KITCHIN'S VOICE: Yeah, nigga. A apple.
SKRAM'S VOICE: What apple?
KITCHIN'S VOICE: I ain't hip.
SKRAM'S VOICE: Can I get a bite?
KITCHIN'S VOICE: It ain't there no more.

SKRAM'S VOICE: It ain't?

KITCHIN'S VOICE: That joint like disappeared, yo.

SKRAM'S VOICE: I feel like I fuckin disappeared.

KITCHIN'S VOICE: Yeah, me, too.

SKRAM'S VOICE: You floatin?

(No answer)

SKRAM'S VOICE: Yo, Kitchin, you floatin?!

KITCHIN'S VOICE: Whatchu think, nigga?!

SKRAM'S VOICE: This shit is bug, right?

(No answer)

SKRAM'S VOICE: It's bug right, Kitchin?

(No answer)

SKRAM'S VOICE: Kitchin!

KITCHIN'S VOICE: Yeah, nigga, it's bug! It's fuckin bug!

(Pause)

SKRAM'S VOICE: Yo, Kitchin, do the Electra got air-conditioning? Cuz I'm hot as a motherfucker...Kitchin!

KITCHIN'S VOICE: *Shshshsh!*

(The sound of creaking in the staircase.)

KITCHIN'S VOICE: You hear that?

SKRAM'S VOICE: I hear it, G.

(The lighting of a match. A cigarette ember burns red.)

SKRAM'S VOICE: Yo, what the fuck is goin on?

(No response)

SKRAM'S VOICE: Kitchin!

KITCHIN'S VOICE: Shut the fuck up, nigga!

SKRAM'S VOICE: Yo, Stargyl! ...Kitchin, where's Stargyl?

ACT TWO

KITCHIN'S VOICE: He over in the corner.

SKRAM'S VOICE: How do you know?

KITCHIN'S VOICE: Cuz I can smell the shit in his pants.

SKRAM'S VOICE: Stargyl, you shit your pants again?

(No response)

SKRAM'S VOICE: Yo, Stargyl!

(No response)

SKRAM'S VOICE: Bark if you can hear me, pussy!

(A single bark)

SKRAM'S VOICE: Stargyl! Stargyl Superstar! …Yo, Kitchin, I'm so hungry it feels like my stomach's maulin my back…I almost ate a fuckin stick today. I was gonna put some mustard on it but I thought about it and shit.

(Slowly, several candles are lit. As the room becomes illuminated, the figures of KITCHIN and SKRAM can be seen dangling from the heavy bag chains. SKRAM is wearing the red pumps. Also, the figure of a MAN can be seen moving throughout the basement. He is eating an apple and smoking a cigarette. He is white, perhaps fiftyish, but ageless somehow. He wears a plain grayish suit. There is a wheelchair parked opposite SKRAM and KITCHIN, a metal suitcase placed next to the wheelchair.)

SKRAM: Yo, who the fuck is that?!

KITCHIN: I ain't hip, B.

(After the MAN finishes lighting all the candles, he takes a seat in the wheelchair and smokes and eats the apple. STARGYL has returned to his shrine of plastic army soldiers. He is now wearing SKRAM's Timberland boots and facing the corner. The back of his pants are soiled.)

SKRAM: *(To the MAN)* Yo.

(No response)

SKRAM: Yo, sir.

(The MAN stares at SKRAM, tilts his head.)

SKRAM: I think that nigga's deaf.

(SKRAM suddenly performs a series of ridiculous hand gestures, an inane attempt at sign language. The MAN continues going about his business.)

SKRAM: Maybe he retarded. *(To the MAN)* Yo, Money, you retarded? Like them niggas in the Tender Olympics.

KITCHIN: *Special* Olympics.

SKRAM: Yeah, them doofy niggas wif the butts on they foreheads.

(The MAN smokes.)

KITCHIN: *(To the MAN)* Scuse me.

(The MAN eats the apple.)

KITCHIN: Um, sir... Yo, scuse me, sir. You the cat from Oswego?

SKRAM: Yeah, G, you the cat from Oswego?

MAN: Well, I don't know.

KITCHIN: You don't know?

SKRAM: Yeah, you don't fuckin know?

MAN: Maybe *you* should tell *me*. Am I the cat from Oswego?

KITCHIN: We askin *you*.

(The MAN smokes.)

KITCHIN: Yo, we asked you a question.

SKRAM: Yeah, we like asked you a question, Money!

MAN: Did you? Is that what that was?

(KITCHIN and SKRAM stare at each other.)

ACT TWO

KITCHIN: Yo, sir, you got a name?

SKRAM: Yeah, you got a fuckin name?!

MAN: I don't know, do I?

KITCHIN: We askin *you*, B.

SKRAM: Yeah, we askin *you*, G!

MAN: Oh, I like this game.

KITCHIN: This ain't no game.

SKRAM: Yeah, G, this ain't no fuckin game!

MAN: A name game. I'm yellow, you're blue, let's walk together at the zoo. Maybe my name starts with a K. Or an S. Or maybe it's fun to guess… Maybe it's *Oz*?

KITCHIN: *Odds?*

SKRAM: As in one, three, five, seven, nine?

KITCHIN: Eleven, thirteen, fifteen, seventeen, nineteen.

SKRAM: You a odd motherfucker, G.

MAN: I'm impressed with your counting ability. But it's *Oz*. With a Z.

KITCHIN: Like Oswald and shit?

SKRAM: Yeah, like that nigga who shot George Washingmachine?

KITCHIN: It's Washing*ton*. And he shot *Kennedy*, knucklehead.

MAN: It's just Oz. Just oh so simply Oz.

KITCHIN: You don't got no last name?

SKRAM: Yeah, G, you don't got no last name?

MAN: As a matter of fact I *do* have a last name.

KITCHIN: Well what is it?

SKRAM: Yeah, G, what the fuck is it?

MAN: Maybe it's Wego?

KITCHIN: Wego.

SKRAM: As in Wego to the post office? Wego to the libary and shit?

MAN: Oz. Wego.

KITCHIN: Oswego.

SKRAM: Oswego.

MAN: You can call me Ozzie.

SKRAM: This shit is definitely bug, yo.

MAN: Or Mr Wego.

KITCHIN: Cool.

SKRAM: Yeah, cool.

(The MAN smokes, exhales.)

MAN: So.

KITCHIN: So what?

SKRAM: Yeah, so the fuck what!?

(The MAN produces a bullhorn.)

MAN: *(Into bullhorn)* What do you think of the rain?

(KITCHIN and SKRAM look at each other.)

MAN: *(Into bullhorn)* Well?

SKRAM: Shit is mad hellefied.

MAN: Hellefied.

SKRAM: Yeah, G. Hellefied.

MAN: Hellefied is a good word. Do you know what it means?

SKRAM: Yeah, I know what that shit means.

MAN: Well, what does it mean?

SKRAM: Like you want a definition?

MAN: Sure.

ACT TWO   39

SKRAM: Seriously?

MAN: *(Into bullhorn)* Oh, I'm deliriously serious.

SKRAM: It means it's some crazy bugged-out shit's what it means. Like it's chasin you and whatnot.

MAN: I would say that's part of it.

SKRAM: Like some mad, over-the-shoulder type nonsense.

MAN: *(Pondering)* Mad, over-the-shoulder type nonsense.

KITCHIN: *(To* SKRAM*)* It means like Hell, knucklehead.

SKRAM: That's basically what I said, G. Like Hell and shit.

MAN: Hellefied rain. A rain of lost and slanted fire: It bleeds down through the soil and finds its passage into nefarious, boiling streams. A cleansing, white-hot rain.

(KITCHIN *and* SKRAM *look at each other. The* MAN *smokes.)*

SKRAM: So Fozzie or Mr Wingo or whatever your name is.

KITCHIN: It's Ozzie, yo.

SKRAM: Fozzie, Kamikaze, Kukla, Fran and Ollie.

KITCHIN: Lemme talk to him, B.

SKRAM: Then talk to him, nigga!

(The MAN *smokes.)*

KITCHIN: Scuse me, Mr Wego, sir. About you bein here and shit. Is we like doin business or what?

MAN: Business?

SKRAM: Yeah, G. *Bidness.*

KITCHIN: Shut the fuck up, Skram!

MAN: What kind of *bid*ness exactly?

KITCHIN: Makin deals. Clockin gees. That general businessy type shit people do.

MAN: Oh, that. Yes, of course. You're talking about. ..

KITCHIN: The girl, yo.

MAN The girl.

SKRAM: Yeah, G, the fuckin girl!

KITCHIN: We doin business, right?

MAN: We are, yes. We are, in fact, in the midst of an all-important transaction. But first things first, it's better not to burst.

KITCHIN: Cool.

SKRAM: Yeah, G, cool.

(The MAN smokes.)

MAN: Cigarette?

KITCHIN: Naw, B.

(MAN offers one to SKRAM.)

SKRAM: Don't smoke squares, G. Hot enough in this motherfucker.

(The MAN smokes.)

KITCHIN: So what's first?

MAN: First?

KITCHIN: You said first things first.

SKRAM: Yeah, G. You said first things first!

MAN: Oh, of course, of course. Well, *first* I'd like to just say that I think those sissy shoes look sensational.

(SKRAM stares down at the pumps.)

SKRAM: Oh, shit!

MAN: *(To SKRAM, into bullhorn)* You show no gratitude.

KITCHIN: Say thank you, Skram.

ACT TWO 41

SKRAM: What?

KITCHIN: Show some gratitude, yo.

SKRAM: Man, fuck you, Kitchin!

MAN: *(Into bullhorn)* Not a good way to start off our bidness relationship.

KITCHIN: Just say it, B!

SKRAM: He tryin to punk me!

KITCHIN: So the fuck what! Just do it, nigga!

(SKRAM *turns to the* MAN.)

SKRAM: Thank you and shit.

MAN: You're welcome·. They make me very glad. They make me want to do a glad dance. A glad dance gives everyone a chance. Have you ever done a glad dance before? It's loads of fun. Shimmy-shimmy cuckoo clock.

SKRAM: Yo, Kitchin, this nigga crazy.

MAN: I'm quite a dancer.

SKRAM: That's pretty bug, yo.

MAN: Bug?

SKRAM: Yeah, bug. Bug as in mad ridickilis.

MAN: Oh, I see—*ridickilis*. And why would my dancing be ridickilis?

SKRAM: Well, you can't be too good at it bein all locked down in that hospital chair. I mean, what the fuck is wrong wif you, G? You got like muscular catastrophe or some shit?

KITCHIN: Muscular *dystrophy*, B.

SKRAM: That joint got a motor?

KITCHIN: *(To* SKRAM*)* Knucklehead!

MAN: You'd be surprised at the amount of work I can get done in this chair.

(SKRAM *revs an imaginary dirt bike.*)

KITCHIN: *(To* SKRAM *) Foolish*-ass nigga!

MAN: If inspired I'm liable to lift right out of it.

SKRAM: *(Mocking)* Woooooooooooooo!

(The MAN *laughs, smokes.)*

MAN: *(To* KITCHIN*)* Can I ask you a question?

SKRAM: *(laughing)* What, you wanna dance? Like we on a telethon and shit?

MAN: That's not what I had in mind. Not yet, anyway.

SKRAM: So whatchu got in mind?

MAN: Well, I was wondering if you were hungry. It doesn't appear that you have much to eat around here.

(KITCHIN *and* SKRAM *stare at each other.*)

MAN: *(Into bullhorn)* Well, are you?

KITCHIN: Yeah, B, we hungry.

MAN: Are you starving? Are your stomachs *mauling your backs*?

KITCHIN: Yeah, B. We starvin. Starvin like Marvin.

MAN: I was just wondering.

KITCHIN: You wonderin?

MAN: Yes. I spend a lot of time wondering. Wonder, wonder, call upon the thunder. Add a pinch of fun and blow it all asunder...so, what do you say, boys, are you hungry?

KITCHIN: Whatchu think, B?

SKRAM: Yeah, G, whatchu think? You see any steaks fryin?

ACT TWO 43

MAN: I'll bet you think about food a lot. The smell of a good meal being prepared.

KITCHIN: Yeah, we think about food. We think about that shit all the time. Why, you givin out hot lunches?

MAN: No, unfortunately I'm not. But I was just *wondering* if one of you hungry fellas wouldn't mind eating a little fish.

KITCHIN: A little fish.

MAN: A small, insignificant fish. *(To* SKRAM*)* You like fish?

SKRAM: Yeah, G. I likes fish. Why, you got some fishsticks or some shit?

MAN: Maybe.

SKRAM: *Maybe.* What the fuck does that mean? You either got fishsticks or you *don't* got fishsticks.

KITCHIN: He talkin about the *fish* fish, yo.

SKRAM: What fish fish?

KITCHIN: The fish in the bucket, B!

MAN: *(To* SKRAM*)* If you eat that fish I'll give you everything in this suitcase.

KITCHIN: And whatchu got in that suitcase?

SKRAM: Yeah, G. Whatchu got in that suitcase, some mad crazy perverted type nonsense? Like four-by-four dildos and whatnot?

(The MAN *opens the suitcase to reveal stacks and stacks of twenty-dollar bills.)*

SKRAM: Oh, shit! Yo, G, you see that?

KITCHIN: I see it, B.

SKRAM: That's like crazy mad bank, yo. Later for that Electra. Fuck around and get a Benz and shit.

MAN: It's all yours.

SKRAM: Word?

MAN: As much as you want.

SKRAM: You hearin this, Kitchin?

KITCHIN: I'm hearin it, yo.

MAN: All you have to do is eat the fish.

SKRAM: Me?

MAN: Yes, you.

SKRAM: Why me?

MAN: Because I choose you, Larry. I think the fish would take to you. If you were a stream it would swim you supreme.

SKRAM: Yo, how did you know—

MAN: Oh, trust me, Larry, I know a lot of things.

SKRAM: So you want me to eat the fish.

MAN: I do, yes.

SKRAM: Like cook that joint up and shit?

MAN: I'd prefer it to be eaten raw.

SKRAM: Raw?

MAN: That is correct, my friend. It would mean more to me that way.

SKRAM: Like cut it up into little parts.

MAN: No. Whole.

SKRAM: The whole fish?

MAN: The fish in its entirety.

SKRAM: Like the fins and the teef and the eyeballs?

MAN: All of it, yes.

SKRAM: Like the insides and the butthole and all the boogies and shit?

MAN: It would be worth quite a sum.

ACT TWO

SKRAM: *(To* KITCHIN *)* This shit is *bananas*, yo.

(STARGYL *crosses to the beach pail, reaches inside, grabs the fish, puts it in his breast pocket, crosses back to his corner.)*

SKRAM: Yo, Stargyl, what the fuck is you doin, G?

(STARGYL *doesn't respond.)*

SKRAM: Stargyl!

MAN: Looks like your friend has other plans.

SKRAM: Put that joint back, yo!—

(STARGYL *doesn't move.)*

SKRAM: Put it back, nigga!

(STARGYL *turns and faces the corner.)*

SKRAM: Yo, let me down, Mr Wiggles.

KITCHIN: Mr *Wego*.

SKRAM: Let me down, Mr Wego, so I can break that nigga's legs.

MAN: Oh, you can't do that.

SKRAM: Whatchu mean I can't do that?

MAN: Things are already set in motion.

SKRAM: You put us up here, didn't you?

MAN: In a manner of speaking, yes.

SKRAM: Stargyl, bring that motherfuckin fish back here, G!

(STARGYL *doesn't move.)*

SKRAM: Bring it back, punk-ass nigga!

(STARGYL *doesn't move.)*

SKRAM: Yo, let me down, Fozzie.

KITCHIN: Ozzie.

SKRAM: Ozzie, c'mon, yo!

MAN: I'll let you down.

SKRAM: You will?

MAN: Under one condition.

SKRAM: What condition?

MAN: That you dance with me.

SKRAM: Dance wif you?

MAN: That's correct.

SKRAM: Like *dance* dance?

MAN: Why, sure.

SKRAM: Like me and you like rumpshakin and shit.

MAN: Word is bond. A little do-si-do.

(SKRAM *turns to* KITCHIN.)

SKRAM: You hearin this, yo?

KITCHIN: I'm hearin it.

SKRAM: *(To the* MAN*)* I dance wif you and what?

MAN: I let you down.

SKRAM: You let me down.

MAN: So you can get the fish.

SKRAM: So I can get the fish.

MAN: So you can eat it.

SKRAM: So I can eat that joint.

MAN: So you can have the money.

(SKRAM *turns to* KITCHIN.)

SKRAM: So we can have the money.

KITCHIN: *(To the* MAN*)* What about the girl?

MAN: Oh, that's right, the girl.

KITCHIN: You still want her, right?

ACT TWO

MAN: Yes. Yes, I do. I want her very much. But I'd really like to dance first.

(SKRAM *turns to* KITCHIN.)

SKRAM: I'm wif that.

MAN: You sure?

SKRAM: Hells yeah. Let me down. I'll dance wif you, G. But you better not try no crazy cumbum pervert shit cuz if I'm forced to I'll break your big ass down.

(*The* MAN *wheels over to* SKRAM, *stands out of the wheelchair, reaches up, effortlessly removes* SKRAM *from the chain, lets him down.* SKRAM *stands awkwardly facing him for a moment.*)

MAN: Perhaps your friend could sing us a little glad song.

(SKRAM *turns to* KITCHIN.)

SKRAM: Sing us a song, G.

MAN: Something with a little life in it.

(KITCHIN *starts to hum a slow spiritual. The* MAN *holds his hand out to* SKRAM.)

MAN: Shall we?

(SKRAM *takes his hand. The* MAN *pulls him close. They slow dance to the spiritual,* SKRAM *still wearing the red pumps. As the song progresses, they draw closer and closer.*)

KITCHIN: *(Singing)*
Florida orange juice on ice
Sounds so nice
In the morning

Florida orange juice on ice
Tastes so fresh
The day is dawning

Florida orange juice
Healthy start
To a brand new day

Florida orange juice
Vitamin C
It's the sunshine way

(KITCHIN *continues to hum while the* MAN *and* SKRAM *continue to dance, slower and slower, until they come to a very dead rest. The* MAN *continues to hold* SKRAM *warmly, staring intently into his eyes.*)

(*The sound of rain. The sound of thunder.*)

MAN: Now go get the fish.

(SKRAM *nods. He crosses to* STARGYL, *who is still turned toward the corner.* SKRAM *turns* STARGYL *around.* STARGYL *clutches his breast pocket.* SKRAM *attempts to pry his hands away.* STARGYL *falls to the floor, still clutching his breast pocket.* SKRAM *strikes him across the face, pries his hands away, thrusts his hands into* STARGYL's *interior breast pocket, steals the fish, crosses back to the* MAN, *turns to* KITCHIN.)

SKRAM: Yo, you want some of this, G?

(KITCHIN *shakes his head.* SKRAM *turns to the* MAN. *The* MAN *makes a gesture to the suitcase fall of money, nods.* SKRAM *raises the fish above his head, lowers it slowly to his lips, swallows the fish whole.*)

(*The* MAN *moves to* SKRAM, *embraces him tenderly for a moment, then guides him to one of the crates, seats him.*)

(*Suddenly, the sound of insects buzzing.* SKRAM *turns to* KITCHIN. SKRAM *You hear that, Kitchin?*)

(KITCHIN *nods. The buzzing swells for a moment.*)

SKRAM: Yo, what is that, G?

(*The* MAN *wheels over to the window, peers up.*)

ACT TWO

MAN: It's the flies.

SKRAM: The flies?

MAN: The din of the rainfly. Such a pretty sound.

(KITCHIN *and* SKRAM *stare at each other, baffled.*)

SKRAM: So, Mr Wego.

MAN: Yes, my little friend.

SKRAM: About the girl…

MAN: The girl. Of course, the girl.

KITCHIN: We should put her back, Skram! Fuck all this nonsense!

MAN: Oh, you don't want to do that.

KITCHIN: We should do it, Skram!

MAN: But it's too late. Things are already set in motion.

KITCHIN: What things?

MAN: Well, the things that matter most, friend. Hasn't anything ever mattered to you? Haven't you always wanted to get on with your life? Get out of this *nowhere-ass ho-infested tizzown*? Think about that.

KITCHIN: Whatchu gonna do with her?

MAN: What am I gonna do with her? There's so much really. So much to do. I could show you if you'd like. Would you like me to show you?

(KITCHIN *nods. The* MAN *crosses to* KITCHIN, *who is still attached to his hook.*)

MAN: I'm going to open my mouth. I'm going to open it as wide as I can. Wider than anything you've ever seen. And when I do, I want you to look inside. Simply look inside and note what you see. What you see is what will be done to her. Now don't close your eyes or you'll miss the surprise.

(KITCHIN *nods. The* MAN *opens, his mouth wide.* KITCHIN *peers inside. A look of terror grows in his face. He starts to scream. After a moment, the* MAN *closes his mouth.)*

MAN: You see?

(KITCHIN *nods. He is hysterical.)*

MAN: *(To* SKRAM*)* I think your friend needs some air. *(To* KITCHIN*)* Would you like some air?

(KITCHIN *nods desperately.)*

(*The* MAN *crosses to* KITCHIN, *frees him from the heavy bag chain, sets him down. The* MAN *takes* KITCHIN's *face in his hands, forces his mouth open, starts to blow into* KITCHIN's *mouth.* KITCHIN *pushes himself away, falls down, quickly gets to his feet, and then makes a dead sprint for the staircase, scrambles up the stairs, exits. Over the following, the* MAN *starts to move from candle to candle, blowing each one out.)*

MAN: So, looks like my business is done.

SKRAM: What about the girl?

MAN: What about her?

SKRAM: Don't you want her and shit?

MAN: I do, son. I do want her.

SKRAM: But you ain't gonna take her wif you?

MAN: No. As a matter of fact, I'm not. Actually, I'm not going to take her with me.

SKRAM: Why not?

MAN: Why not?

SKRAM: Yeah, G, why the fuck not? You came all this way. Oswego's like a forty-five-minute drive and shit.

MAN: Oh, I don't drive. I fly. Everywhere. Over the hills. Over the dells. Over the firelight. I rarely use my

ACT TWO

legs. That's why I have such a hard time walking. My work is done. She's all yours now.

SKRAM: I don't want that little ho.

MAN: Oh, but I think you do.

SKRAM: What the fuck am I sposed to do wif her?

(After the MAN *finishes blowing out the last candle, he starts to leave. Just as he reaches the foot of the stairs:)*

SKRAM: Yo, I don't want her, Ozzie!

(The MAN *stops, turns.)*

MAN:
Once long ago there was a boy named Larry.
Not Johnny or Dellwood or Gerald or Gary.
He was bright as the sky and shiny as tin.
He had a mother so fat, and a brother so thin.

They lived in a house on Blueberry Lane.
A house made of bread and old candycane.

Mother was sad, her face long as the Nile.
It showed in her eyes and her upside-down smile.

She was hungry as mice but there was nothing to eat.
Not a speck in the fridge, not a crumb on the street.

Then one day she started eating the walls!
After all they were bread,
not stone nor brick stalls.
She thought, The wall in the kitchen
'might taste pretty good.
It might be delicious! I should eat it, I should!

So she ate through the wall, she made a big hole.
She had to act fast, the boys couldn't know.
She looked through the hole and what did she see?
People to know and places to be!

She could fly to Japan or sail in a boat!
She could jump in the sea and just simply float!

She could go catch a bird or climb a tall tree!
There were horses and spaceships and magic T V!

That night while the boys were sleeping and dreaming
she jumped through the wall and ran away screaming.

Beyond the Old Sea. Past the last train.
Far from their house on Blueberry Lane.

When Larry awakened he searched for their mother.
It was high time to feed his big baby brother.
She wasn't here. She wasn't there.
She wasn't up or down.
Mommy! Larry called, but Mommy couldn't be found.

A month went by. And then two more.
And then another—that made four!

It was scary
but Larry was brave as a bear.
But the food was all gone, they couldn't eat air.

So just like their mother,
they began eating the house.
They nibbled it raw with the speed of a mouse.
Walls made of bread—still a couple of those.
One by the sink and one by the stove.

But after a while there was nothing but holes.
Nothing but holes for the wind and the crows.

So they left their old place on Blueberry Lane.
They walked to the railroad and counted the trains.

They washed in the river, slept under trees,
ate beetles and snowballs and old dirty leaves.

(*The* MAN *hands a tube of glue to* SKRAM, *gently seats him in the wheelchair.*)

MAN:
One day in June they saw a woman walk by.
Did she look familiar! Familiar, oh my!

ACT TWO 53

She was fat as a whale and, my, did she wiggle!
She waddled so fast, her whole body jiggled.

Momma! Larry screamed. *It's Mommy! It's Mother!*
She's come back to get us, Big Baby Brother!

Larry knelt down and prayed at her feet.
Mommy, oh Mommy. Dear Mommy My Sweet.
Where did you go?! We've had nothing to eat.

He hugged her and squeezed her; and tickled her nose.
He kissed her fat legs, all ten of her toes.
But Mommy was hungry, she had nothing for Larry.
She kicked him, slapped him, and goddamn it was scary.

Poor little Larry lay heaped in the road.
And his miserable heart shrank small as a toad.
Big Baby Brother couldn't utter a sound:
his tongue had gone still as a stump in the ground.
Mommy!, he tried, but nothing was said.
And since that sad day, his poor voice was dead.

(SKRAM *starts to cry.*)

MAN:
Away Mother walked, fat as a hog.
Big Baby Brother lay long as a log.
It was getting so late, there was nowhere to go.
There would be rain and cold wind and blizzards of snow.

Their stomachs would howl
and where would they sleep?
It was a sad little time.
Too sad to weep.

(*The* MAN *embraces* SKRAM *tenderly.* SKRAM *continues crying.*)

(*The* MAN *takes* SKRAM's *face in his hands and kisses his mouth for a long moment. They both keep their eyes open. It is a transaction more than anything sexual.*)

MAN: Go to her, my little friend. Simply go to her. You'll know what to do. *(He crosses to his things, slowly gathers his wheelchair, folds it, leaves the suitcase fall of money. He ascends the stairs with his wheelchair, exits.)*

*(*SKRAM *takes off the pumps, sprints halfway up the stairs, looks, runs back down the stairs, sprints to the window, peers out, jumps down, then starts to pace around the room. His pacing gains velocity, like that of a wild animal trapped in a cage. After a moment he crosses to* STARGYL, *stands over him for a moment, drags him out from behind his shrine of plastic army men.* STARGYL *attempts to get away.* SKRAM *kicks him in the face, then starts to beat him on the floor. It ends with* SKRAM *kicking* STARGYL *in the ribs.* STARGYL *is crouched in the center of the basement, his hands shielding his head.* SKRAM *reaches under* STARGYL'S *shirt and removes the shoelace necklace with the key, then the revolver from his leg.* SKRAM *crosses to the entrance to the boiler room, inserts the key, turns it, removes the lock. He opens the door, stands in the entrance for a long moment. He then unscrews the top to the glue, snorts it, staggers a bit, drops the tube of glue, enters the boiler room, leaving the door open.)*

(The sound of loud thunder. The sound of flies buzzing. Two gunshots. The faint sound of fire crackling.)

*(*STARGYL *slowly rises off the floor, crosses back to his corner, stands. The sound of the flies buzzing grows louder. Slow footfalls can be heard descending the stairs. Moments later,* KITCHIN *appears. He is drenched from the rain and there are ruptured flies all over his football jersey. He is holding a large, white offertory candle, a small flame burning at the top. He stands very still for a moment.)*

KITCHIN: The flies is everywhere, Stargyl. Like pepper falling from the sky. Buzzin all in your mouth. Your eyes. The holes in your nose.

ACT TWO

I run over to Saint Jack's. Run like there's rain burnin through my blood. Never run so fast in my life. My legs is just goin wild. Think if I run fast enough it'll make that wind leave my stomach. Make them cats stop cryin.

I get to Saint Jack's and everyone's gone. No priest. Nobody in the pews. Not even no birds swoopin down. Thought niggas might be standin in fronta the fans. Thought the flies woulda drove folks inside. But it was mad empty, yo. The way shit is empty when all you can hear is the sound of your own blood movin through you. The blue Jesus just starin back at you like he hungry.

So I scream. I'm like, "Where's everybody at?!" I'm like, "Yo, God! Yo, God, where is you, G?!" But there ain't no answer. Only the sound of them flies buzzin. So I grab a candle. Big white one right off the altar. And I set Saint Jack's on fire, Stargyl. The cross. The pews. All the pictures. Fire burns up the walls like little hands runnin. Windows pop. Flames shoot right through the roof.

Thought God would see it. Hear them windows poppin. See them birds burnin. Somethin. But God didn't hear nothin, Stargyl. Like that shit didn't even happen. It's like that nigga's asleep.

(The faint sound of fire crackling.)

(SKRAM appears in the entrance to the boiler room, holding the revolver. His eyes are huge, ghostly.)

SKRAM: Hey, Kitchin… You ready to break north and shit?

(No response)

SKRAM: Let's go, yo. Get the fuck outta here. Just you and me, G.

(SKRAM points to STARGYL.)

SKRAM: Leave that nigga here.

(KITCHIN *doesn't move.*)

SKRAM: C'mon, Kitchin.

KITCHIN: doesn't move.

SKRAM: What's up, G?

(KITCHIN *doesn't move.*)

SKRAM: You ain't comin?

KITCHIN shakes his head.

SKRAM: You ain't?

(KITCHIN *shakes his head.*)

SKRAM: Yo, you know that shit Ozzie showed you. That shit that was in his mouth?

(KITCHIN *nods.*)

SKRAM: Well, I got it now. See?

(SKRAM *opens his mouth very wide and shows* KITCHIN. KITCHIN *is filled with sorrow.* SKRAM *closes his mouth.*)

SKRAM: Pretty dope, right? You want some?

(KITCHIN *shakes his head.*)

SKRAM: You sure?

(*No response*)

SKRAM: Punk-ass nigga.

(SKRAM *crosses to* STARGYL, *pulls his Timberland boots off of* STARGYL's *feet, puts them back on, crosses to the suitcase, closes it, grabs the handle.* SKRAM *crosses to the staircase, ascends the stairs slowly.* SKRAM *stops, turns to* STARGYL.)

SKRAM: Yo, Stargyl, you see Mommy tell her I said she a ho.

(SKRAM *exits up the stairs with the suitcase. The light starts to flicker.*)

ACT TWO

(STARGYL *crosses to the center of the room with the milk carton boat, sets it down, then crosses the entrance to the boiler room, exits.* KITCHIN *crosses to the center of the room, sets the offertory candle down, kneels beside it.*)

(STARGYL *re-enters with a life-sized little girl doll cradled in his arms. She is dressed identically to the* GIRL *who visited* STARGYL *toward the end of ACT ONE. Her eyes have been shot out.* STARGYL *sets her in the milk carton on the floor.* KITCHIN *starts to weep.* STARGYL *grabs the beach pail, places* KITCHIN's *hand in the water.*)

STARGYL: *(Singing)*
Florida orange juice on ice
Sounds so nice
In the morning

Florida orange juice on ice
Tastes so fresh
The day is dawning

Florida orange juice
Healthy start
To a brand new day

Florida orange juice
Vitamin C
It's the sunshine way

(*Lights fade as* STARGYL *swirls the water around* KITCHIN's *hand. The sound of fire can be heard crackling in the streets.*)

END OF PLAY

www.ingramcontent.com/pod-product-compliance
Lightning Source LLC
Chambersburg PA
CBHW060220050426
42446CB00013B/3119